PRAIRIE

Bluestem grassland, Chase County, Kansas, 31 October 1979.

TERRY EVANS

PRAIRIE

IMAGES OF GROUND AND SKY

Introductory Essays by Wes Jackson and Gregory Bateson

 UNIVERSITY PRESS OF KANSAS

Published by the University Press of Kansas (Lawrence, Kansas 66045), which was organized
by the Kansas Board of Regents and is operated and funded by Emporia State University,
Fort Hays State University, Kansas State University, Pittsburg State University, the
University of Kansas, and Wichita State University

Library of Congress Cataloging in Publication Data: see page 72

Publication was made possible by grants from The Fourth National Bank & Trust Co.
Charitable Trust, Wichita, Kansas; John Simpson, Fairway, Kansas; Range Oil Company, Inc.,
Wichita, Kansas; and Smith Ranch, Latham, Kansas.

Albrecht Durer painting (p. 12) used by permission of Graphische Sammlung,
Albertina, Vienna.

Dedicated to the Prairie

PREFACE

These photographs were all made with a Hasselblad 500/CM camera, using for the most part a 50mm lens and occasionally a 60mm lens. A 150mm lens, sometimes with extension ring, was often used to photograph animals and birds. All photographs were taken between spring 1978 and spring 1985. All are of unplowed prairie, including an 80-acre piece of virgin prairie just north of Salina, Kansas, owned by Nick and Joyce Fent; portions of the Flint Hills of Kansas; the Weaver Prairie near Lincoln, Nebraska; the 8,616-acre Konza Prairie managed by Kansas State University of Manhattan, Kansas; and the Maxwell Game Preserve near Roxbury, Kansas.

I wish to express thanks to many people who have helped with my work of thinking about and seeing the prairie: to Sam, my husband (and best friend), and to David and Corey, our children, who affirmed and supported this work always; to Nick and Joyce Fent, who gave me a key to the gate to their 80 acres of prairie and who taught me where to look and when, according to the schedule of the prairie; to Wes Jackson, who introduced me to the prairie in the first place and who first told me why the prairie matters; to Dana Jackson, Kelly Kindscher, and Jim Peterson, who shared with me much thought and care about the nature of the prairie; to Lee Schoenburg, for encouragement and interest that encompass all aspects of this work; to Norman Geske, Andy Grundberg, Saralyn Reece Hardy, Robert Morton, Peter Schlessinger, and Tom Southall, for artistic response and encouragement; to the late Gregory Bateson, whose work challenges me to be both rigorous and loving; and to the staff of the University Press of Kansas, for patience and diligence. There are many people whom I haven't named who have helped me in diverse ways. Some have assisted me with plant identification; some have led me to find prairie wildlife; and others have given me insights and information. I am indebted to those people.

CONTENTS

AN INTRODUCTION

Living Nets in a New Prairie Sea

by Wes Jackson

The difference between a wheat field and the prairie is clear to scientist and artist alike. For the scientist, the first considerations are biological and involve the most rock-bottom basics of ecology. The artist picks up the reflections of these differences in ensemble, emphasizing the aesthetic level. But anyone who goes beyond the superficial differences between farm fields and the ancient grassland knows two things. The first is that the prairie builds and protects soil, while agriculture erodes it and wears it out. The second is that the future of the human experiment depends not only on our collective understanding of the ecological basics but also on our caring enough to develop a truly sustainable agriculture.

What are these differences from an ecological point of view? Most obvious, perhaps, is the fact that the prairie emphasizes a mixture of plants—as the ecologist would say, polyculture. The human, over most of the landscape, struggles to maintain monocultures. The next most obvious fact is that the prairie features perennial plants while agriculture features annuals. The prairie's longevity resides in the roots. Though the above-ground parts of the prairie's perennials may die back each year, the roots are immortal. Whether those sun-cured leaves, passed over by the buffalo in the fall migration, go quickly in a lightning-started prairie fire or, as is more often the case, slowly by the smokeless fires of decay, the roots hold fast what they have earned from rock and subsoil. Whichever way these top parts burn, with smoke or without, the perennial roots will soon capture and save most of the briefly-free nutrients for a living future. And so an alliance of soil and perennial root, well adapted to the task of blotting up a drenching rain, reincarnates last year's growth. Soil does run to the sea in nature's sytem, as it did in the beginning before land plants appeared, but gravity's influence can't compete with this nutrient recharge and the holding power of the living net created by nosing roots of dalea, pasqueflower, and bluestem.

Species diversity breeds dependable chemistry. The above-ground diversity of the prairie has a multiplier effect on the seldom-seen, teeming diversity below. Bacteria, fungi, and invertebrates live out their lives reproducing by the power of sun-sponsored photons captured in the green molecular traps set above. If we could adjust our eyes to a power beyond that of the electron microscope, we would find ourselves reeling in a seemingly surrealistic universe of exchanging ions where water molecules dominate and where colloidal clay plates are held in position by organic thread molecules, which, important though they may be in a larger scheme, are regarded as just another meal by innumerable microscopic invertebrates. The action begins when roots decay and above-ground residues break down and the released nutrients begin their downward tumble through soil catacombs to start all over again. And we who stand above in thoughtful examination, all the while smelling and rolling fresh soil between our fingers and thumbs, distill these myriads of action into one concept—soil health or balance—and leave it at that.

Agriculture coasts on the accumulated principal and interest hard-earned by nature's life forms over those millions of years of adjustment to dryness, fire, and grinding ice. Lately agriculture has been coasting on the sunlight trapped by floras long extinct. We pump it, process it, and transport it over the countryside as chemicals and inject it into our wasting fields as chemotherapy. Then we watch the fields respond with an unsurpassed vigor, and we feel informed on the subject of agronomics. That we can feed billions is less a sign of nature's renewable bounty and our knowledge and more a sign of her forgiveness and our discount of the future. For how opposite could the annual condition in monoculture be from what nature prefers? Roots and above-ground parts alike die every year, so through much of the calendar the mechanical grip on the soil must rely on death rather than life. Mechanical disturbance, powered by an ancient flora, imposed by a mined metal, may make weed control effective, but the farm far from weatherproof. In the course of it all, soil compacts, crumb structure declines, soil porosity decreases, and the wick effect for pulling moisture down into the soil diminishes. Monoculture means a decline in the range of invertebrate and microbial forms. Microbial specialists with narrow enzyme systems make such specific demands that just any old crop won't do. We do manage some diversity through crop rotation, but from the point of view of various microbes, it is a poor substitute for the greater diversity that prevailed on the prairie. Monoculture means that botanical and hence chemical diversity above ground is also absent. This invites epidemics of pathogens or epidemic grazing by insect populations free to spend most of their energy reproducing, eating, and growing. Insects are better controlled if they are forced to spend a good portion of their energy budget buzzing around hunting, among many species in a polyculture, for the plants they have evolved to eat.

Some of the activity found in the untilled sod can be found in the human-managed fields, but plowing has sharply reduced many of these soil qualities. Had too much been destroyed, of course, we would not have food today. But then who can say that our great grandchildren will have it a hundred years from now? It is hard to say exactly what happened when the living net was ripped apart, when the wisdom that the prairie had accumulated over the millions of years was forgotten in favor of the simpler more human-directed system.

So where does all this leave us? Is there any way to return to a system that is at once self-renewing like the prairie or forest and yet capable of supporting the current and expanding human population? I think that breeding new crops from native plants selected from nature's abundance and stimulating the presettlement botanical complexity of a region should make it easier for us to solve many agricultural problems.

As civilizations have flourished, many upland landscapes that supported them have died, leaving behind desert and mud-flat wastelands. But as it happened, civilizations passed on accumulated knowledge to their successors, and we can say without exaggeration that these wastelands are the price paid for the accumulated knowledge. In our century this knowledge has grown enormously, and on balance it seems arrogant to ignore it, for it has restorative potential. The goal of developing a truly sustainable food supply could stimulate a trend exactly opposite to that which we have followed on the globe since we stepped onto the agricultural treadmill some ten millennia ago.

Aldo Leopold lamented that "no living man will see the long-grass prairie, where a sea of prairie flowers lapped at the stirrups of the pioneer." Many share his lament, for what is left are prairie islands far too small to be counted as a "sea." Essentially all this vast region, a million square miles, was turned under to make our corn belt and breadbasket. But now the grandchildren of the pioneers have the opportunity to establish a new sea of perennial prairie flowers, the product of accumulated scientific knowledge, their own cleverness, and the wisdom of the prairie.

The Prairie Seen Whole

by Gregory Bateson

Terry Evans's book on the prairie is what is called a sign of the times, and I hope that means that it is a sign of good times to come. We have not since the sixteenth century had artists whose prime direction was the synthesis between a scientific and an aesthetic understanding of nature. There have been romantic attempts at this among French Impressionists and such landscape artists as old Crome and Cotman and Constable, but to approach the two sides of the living thing with equal imagination and discipline has almost never been attempted. The trouble seems to be that the world to be investigated is commonly split into two sides—the mechanical and the aesthetic—and the human mind, the organ to which is assigned the task of synthesizing these two sides, is itself correspondingly split between imagination and rigor. There is always a temptation to apply the rigor of the mind to the scientific view of nature while the poetic imagination licks its lips over the elegancies of growth.

So, escaping these traps, this book goes back to Albrecht Dürer in the sixteenth century to try to tell the reader what it is all about, and there is no reason to doubt that Dürer was Terry Evans's sort of person. One thinks of the portrait of a tuft of grass and the drawing in the British Museum of a stag beetle, which I suppose Dürer never saw alive. Of course the stag beetle is dead and anybody who is familiar with live stag beetles will see at once that he is a little rotten in the joints, and the tuft of grass, while enormously ambitious, fails as a representational work.

It is the marriage between art and representation that is necessary in this business, and this book attempts to combine rigorous photography with love of the prairie.

It is common today to regret that Renaissance Man is extinct like the Dodo. In the academic world I often meet those who think what constituted the Renaissance scholar was mastery of many disciplines, and every university has so-called interdisciplinary projects that try to create the spirit of Renaissance Man. I think, however, that what is extinct is the creative man who will precisely combine scientific rigor with imagination. It is this combination that is extinct, and I begin to hope that the science of ecology may do much to bring it back. It is in this sense that I regard Terry Evans's book as a sign of better times to come. She brings both love and precision to her analysis.

Prairie Patterns

by Terry Evans

I never intended to photograph the prairie. For years I had photographed people and assumed that anything I needed to learn could come from being in and observing human relationships. When some friends asked me to photograph some survey work they were doing on a nearby prairie, I agreed out of friendship, not out of interest in the prairie. One day on the prairie, while my friends worked, I wandered around looking, and suddenly I began to see the ground. The realization came that I could stand in one spot and look at the ground for at least an hour and still not see everything happening at my feet. I started to photograph the prairie ground.

Then I began to learn the flowers and the grasses, with names like poems, silverleaf scurfpea, catclaw sensitive brier, nodding lady's tresses, green antelopehorn, rayless thelesperma, mugwort wormwood. I felt embarrassed when I came across one whose name I'd forgotten or hadn't yet learned; it was like slighting a friend. Earlier on the prairie, the plains Indians had respectfully learned as much as possible about a plant in order to deserve to call it by name and to use it for food, medicinal, or ritualistic purposes.

I began to see the difference between prairie and adjacent wheat fields. The prairie is a polyculture of perennial plants, while the wheat field is a monoculture of annuals. The prairie expresses a cyclical or spiral system of growth based on diversity and self-renewal, while the wheat field expresses a linear system of growth based on uniformity and leading to exhaustion. The prairie, unlike the shallow-rooted wheat field, has roots that often extend twenty-five feet into the earth, holding the soil firm. Of the entire biomass of the prairie, only 15 percent is visible above ground; the other 85 percent lies below the surface. I was awed by this fact as I observed the tremendous diversity and complexity of grasses and forbs visible at my feet. The rich variety of texture and color and line was stimulating but chaotic. I found it impossible to discern any visual order or pattern of organization as I observed the ground, but I was convinced that a pattern must be there. I believed that if I only looked long enough and hard enough, I would eventually be able to see the pattern and thus to understand the prairie.

Whenever I was on the prairie, I experienced a kind of presence I had not felt anywhere else. It mystified me. Was the prairie holy? I came across some clues in these words by Thomas Merton: "The more a tree is like itself, the more it is like Him. If it tried to be like something else, which it was never intended to be, it would be less like God and therefore it would give him less glory. No two created beings are exactly alike and their individuality is no imperfection. On the contrary, the perfection of each created thing is not merely in its conformity to an abstract type, but in its own individual identity with itself." The prairie was simply being what it was meant to be, and in being itself it was being holy.

I learned that in Greek and Hebrew, wind is the same word as spirit and breath, and I began to understand something else about the nature of the holy because I could see the effects of the wind but not the wind itself. I noticed how the wind changed the colors of the grasses as it wove them together, and moved them in rhythms of line, and I saw a tangle of winter prairie grass making spare calligraphy in the wind.

I began to see many spirals on the prairie, which emphasized for me the cyclical system of nature. William Irwin Thompson says that the ego is a line and the soul is a circle "but the archetypal image of the resolution of the line and the circle is the spiral, for the spiral is the basic image of dynamic growth. . . . The spiral expresses movement that includes as it unfolds." The bristles of the porcupine grass become spiral springs and as the plant matures and dries, the humidity change causes the tension of the spring to expand and contract, and as this motion occurs, the spiral drills the seed into the ground. The center of the black Sampson forms a spiral swirl and the blossoms of the blue wild indigo and the nodding lady's tresses form spiral configurations around their stalk, as the sequence conforms to the mathematical Fibonacci series. Wild gourd and wild bean vines spiral across the ground, and the blossoms of the morning glory spiral forth as they unfold.

One day in April I took a picture of some sage coming through the grass, and the plants were in a sort of spiral configuration of sage, old straw grass, and new grass. As I looked at the photographic image later, the sage looked like stars and the grass like a galaxy, and suddenly I realized that the sky was a part of the prairie too. I began to point my lens at the sky with the dawning awareness "as above, so below." When I photographed the prairie from a plane at about 1,000 feet, I was amazed at how similar the macro and the micro patterns were.

Gradually, I was learning about the form of the prairie, and as I learned about the form, I was being initiated into the mysteries of form in art and life. I began to understand that sacred and symbolic knowledge, knowledge that goes beyond the world of appearances, is transmitted through form and structure.

My photographs of the ground displayed a flat planar structure, unlike landscape images based on one-point perspective, the lenslike system of drawing developed around the time of the Renaissance. I began to understand that pre-Renaissance art (such as Egyptian hieroglyphics, Chinese calligraphic drawings, Persian miniatures, Greek icon paintings, European cave paintings, and Native American petroglyphs) that had used flat overall nonlinear, nonlens configurations was able to carry more symbolism about the experience of reality than lenslike expressions. This was true partly because the form itself expressed a spatial awareness that went beyond the world of appearances.

The sixteenth-century German artist, Albrecht Dürer, surely believed the same thing, as seen in his renderings of plants. Although Dürer was partly responsible for the device of linear perspective, he was not limited to its use. As seen in his circular astrological maps and mandala embroidery patterns, Dürer recognized that his questions about the nature of the universe had broader answers than those defined by any particular perceptual device. He was perhaps, also looking for the interrelationships in nature which he could not see, but which he suspected were there. Dürer would surely have enjoyed playing with the lens perceptions of a camera today.

As I looked at the forbs and grasses, continually searching for information about pattern and form, I believe that I had accidentally entered into a relationship with the prairie, considerably less developed than but similar to the relationship expressed by the plains Indians long before me in their daily life and in their rock art. In paying careful attention to the plants around them, they were living daily in two orders of reality—one of appearances and one beyond appearances. Their petroglyphs, in their structure and form, were maps of their spiritual universe revealing dimensions beyond the physical, arrived at through focus on the physical. Barney Mitchell, Navaho, says, "The greatest sacred thing is knowing the order and structure of things."

The prairie had been bringing up many questions for me about the nature of form in visual expression, the shape of space, the nature of the sacred, agriculture, the significance of learning the plants, and more. The prairie expressed metaphors for human community about living with diversity and deep roots and a sense of place. Sometimes I seem to be coming full circle, but the circle becomes a spiral as I continue working to render images of the patterns of the prairie.

What pattern connects the crab to the lobster and the orchid to the primrose and all four of them to me? And me to you? And all the six of us to the amoeba in one direction and to the back-ward schizophrenic in another?

What is the pattern which connects all the living creatures?

—Gregory Bateson, *Mind and Nature*

Daisy fleabane, asters, mixed prairie grasses, and cheat grass, Fent's Prairie, Salina, Kansas, 24 June 1978.

Fent's Prairie edge, 4 October 1978 (top left);   Horse Thief Canyon, Kanopolis Lake, Kansas, 21 March 1979 (top right);
Fent's Prairie, 27 March 1979 (bottom left);   Fent's Prairie, 11 October 1978 (bottom right).

18

Nodding lady's tresses, dropseed and other grasses, Fent's Prairie, 22 October 1978 (top right);
Horse Thief Canyon, 20 March 1979 (top left);   Pheasant feathers, Fent's Prairie, 11 November 1978 (bottom left);
Prairie dropseed, near Salina, March 1984 (bottom right).

I wonder if the ground has anything to say? I wonder if the ground is listening to what is said? I wonder if the ground would come alive and what is on it? Though I hear what the ground says. The ground says, it is the Great Spirit that placed me here. The Great Spirit tells me to take care of the Indians, to feed them aright. The Great Spirit appointed the roots to feed the Indians on. The water says the same thing. The Great Spirit directs me. Feed the Indians well. The grass says the same thing. Feed the Indians well. The ground, water and grass say, The Great Spirit has given us our names. We have these names and hold these names. The ground says, the Great Spirit has placed me here to produce all that grows on me, trees and fruit. The same way the ground says, it was from me man was made. The Great Spirit, in placing men on the earth, desired them to take good care of the ground and to do each other no harm.

    —Young Chief of the Cayuses, *Touch The Earth* (1855)

Konza Prairie, near Manhattan, Kansas, May 1979.

Konza Prairie, June 1982.

So many species—often a total of 200 or more per square mile—can exist together only by sharing the soil at different levels, by obtaining light at different heights, and by making maximum demands for water, nutrients, and light at different seasons of the year. Legumes add nitrogen to the soil; tall plants protect the lower ones from the heating and drying effects of full insolation; and the matformers and other prostrate species further reduce water loss by covering the soil's surface, living in an atmosphere that is much better supplied with moisture than are the windswept plants above them. Light is absorbed at many levels; the more-or-less-vertical leaves of the dominant grasses permit light to filter between them as the sun swings across the heaven.

—John E. Weaver, *Prairie Plants and Their Environment*

Sage, Scribner's panic grass, and other native grasses, Fent's Prairie, May 1979.

Thunderstorm clouds over Ottawa County, Kansas, July 1982.

Silverleaf scurfpea and grasses, Fent's Prairie, June 1979.

Butterfly milkweed, Konza Prairie, July 1984.

Poppy mallow, Fent's Prairie, June 1978.

Leadplant, Konza Prairie, July 1979.

Horse Thief Canyon, October 1981.

Sky over Topeka, Kansas, September 1979.

Sky over Salina, Kansas, August 1979.

Sky seen from plane over Salina, Kansas, December 1980.

Bison at Maxwell Game Preserve, Roxbury, Kansas, December 1981.

The earth was warm under me, and warm as I crumbled it through my fingers. Queer little red bugs came out and moved in slow squadrons around me. Their backs were polished vermilion, with black spots. I kept as still as I could. Nothing happened. I did not expect anything to happen. I was something that lay under the sun and felt it, like the pumpkins, and I did not want to be anything more, I was entirely happy. Perhaps we feel like that when we die and become a part of something entire, whether it is sun and air, or goodness and knowledge. At any rate, that is happiness; to be dissolved into something complete and great. When it comes to one, it comes as naturally as sleep.

—Willa Cather, *My Antonia*

Mixed prairie grasses, Konza Prairie, September 1979.

Ottawa County, Kansas, October 1982.

Konza Prairie containing switchgrass, Indian grass, big bluestem, side oats, grama and other grasses, October 1980.

Saline County, Kansas, March 1983.

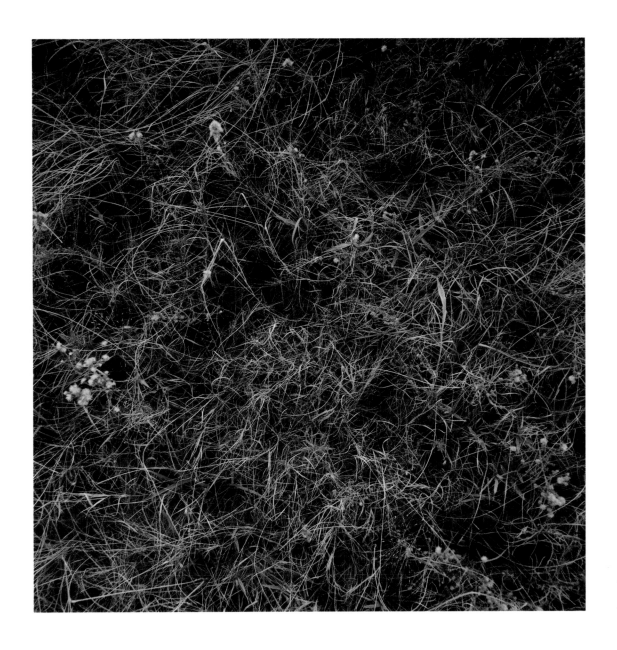

Asters, three awn, dropseed, and other grasses, Fent's Prairie, November 1979.

An atom at large in the biota is too free to know freedom; an atom back in the sea has forgotten it. For every atom lost to the sea, the prairie pulls another out of the decaying rocks. The only certain truth is that its creatures must suck hard, live fast, and die often, lest its losses exceed its gains.

—Aldo Leopold, "Odyssey," *The Sand County Almanac*

White-tailed deer skull, Fent's Prairie, June 1978.

Konza Prairie, February 1979.

Bison fur, Ottawa County, Kansas, August 1982.

Maxwell Game Preserve, March 1982.

Plants are powerful and harbor many secrets.
Our lives are bound up with the plant world
far more tightly than any of us might imagine.

—Tom Robbins, *Even Cowgirls Get the Blues*

Goldenrod and grasses, Fent's Prairie, 28 March 1979.

Leadplant and mixed grasses, Fent's Prairie, June 1979.

Leadplant, prairie dropseed, and compass plant,
prairie near Lawrence, Kansas, July 1980.

Blue wild indigo, Fent's Prairie, July 1979.

Mixed prairie grasses, Weaver Prairie,
Lincoln, Nebraska, October 1981.

After ice storm, near Salina, Kansas, February 1982.

Swainson's hawk, Saline County, Kansas, December 1981.

Storm lifting near Concordia, Kansas, October 1980.

Sky over southern Nebraska, October 1980.

Rose verbena and prairie parsley, Camp Hammond, near Topeka, Kansas, April 1982.

Packard's grasshopper on Indian grass, Saline County, Kansas, September 1982.

Switch grass and others, Konza Prairie, July 1979.

Bison, Maxwell Game Preserve, Roxbury, Kansas, December 1981.

Western harvest mouse, Ottawa County, Kansas, July 1981.

Konza Prairie, October 1982.

Konza Prairie, January 1985.

Over the elevated lands and prairie bluffs, where the grass is thin and short, the fire slowly creeps with a feeble flame, which one can easily step over; where the wild animals often rest in their lairs until the flames almost burn their noses, when they will reluctantly rise and leap over it, and trot off amongst the cinders, where the fire has passed and left the ground as black as jet.

—George Catlin, *Letters and Notes on the Manners, Customs, and Conditions of North American Indians* (1832)

But if there was wind, there was fire blizzard—one of the greatest horrors of prairie life.

It came with walls of flame 30 feet high and a deep devouring roar, and black smoke instead of white, and the sun darkened and animals went mad. The flow of these great prairie fires could be seen for 40 miles and showers of ash and flake would be carried that far ahead by the wind. Single prairie fires were known to have burned more than 200 square miles, and one fire traveled over 22 miles ''as fast as a horse could run.''

—John Madson, *Where the Sky Begins* (1982)

Prairie burn, Lake Melvern, south of Lyndon, Kansas, April 1981.

Lake Melvern, April 1981.

Maxwell Game Preserve, April 1982.

Maxwell Game Preserve, April 1982.

Clouds over the prairie, August 1980.

Konza Prairie after spring burning, June 1979.

Native prairie bunch grass after a burn, Saline County, Kansas, May 1982.

Fairy ring of mixed grasses and brome, with daisy fleabane blooming outside the ring, Fent's Prairie, June 1979.

Milk snake, University of Kansas Environmental Laboratory north of Lawrence, Kansas, May 1982.

The prairie is a symbol of everyday life.

—Hyemeyohsts Storm, *Seven Arrows*

Sky over Shawnee County, Kansas, September 1979.

Konza Prairie, June 1982.

The average aboveground biomass of the prairie, inclusive of live, standing dead and litter, was 275 grams per square meter, and the average belowground, 1625 grams per square meter. Percentagewise this means that roughly 15 percent of the total standing crop occurs above ground, and 85 percent, below ground.

—P. L. Sims and J. S. Singh, "Preliminary Analysis of Structure and Function on Grasslands," *Prairie: A Multiple View*

Describing people who do not know where the true springs of secret powers lie, an ancient adept says: "Worldly people lose the roots and cling to the tree tops."

—C. G. Jung

Prairie roots and big bluestem and other grasses, Konza Prairie, October 1979.

Common Prairie Plants

Aromatic aster *(Aster oblongifolius)*
Baldwin ironweed *(Vernonia baldwinii)*
Beardtongue *(Penstemon cobaea)*
Black Sampson *(Echinacea angustifolia)*
Blazing star *(Liatris punctata)*
Blue-eyed grass *(Sisyrinchium campestre)*
Blue verbena *(Verbena hastata)*
Blue wild indigo *(Baptisia australis)*
Bluntleaf milkweed *(Asclepias amplexicaulis)*
Bracted spiderwort *(Tradescantia bracteata)*
Breadroot scurfpea *(Psoralea esculenta)*
Bush morning-glory *(Ipomoea leptophylla)*
Butterfly milkweed *(Asclepias tuberosa)*
Cancer-root *(Orobanche uniflora)*
Carolina anemone *(Anemone caroliniana)*
Carolina geranium *(Geranium carolinianum)*
Carolina horsenettle *(Solanum carolinense)*
Carrotleaf lomatium *(Lomatium daucifolium)*
Catclaw sensitive brier *(Schrankia nuttalli)*
Clammy groundcherry *(Physalis heterophylla)*
Clove currant *(Ribes odoratum)*
Columnar prairie coneflower *(Ratibida columnifera)*
Common evening primrose *(Oenothera villosa)*
Common goldenrod *(Solidago missouriensis)*
Common milkweed *(Asclepias syriaca)*
Common prickly pear *(Opuntia macrorhiza)*
Common sunflower *(Helianthus annuus)*
Common yarrow *(Achillea millefolium)*
Compass plant *(Silphium laciniatum)*
Creeping Whitlow grass *(Draba reptans)*
Cutleaf evening primrose *(Oenothera laciniata)*
Cutleaf ironplant *(Haplopappus spinulosus)*
Daisy fleabane *(Erigeron strigosus)*
Dwarf dandelion *(Krigia dandelion)*
Ellisia *(Ellisia nyctelea)*
Fendler aster *(Aster fendleri)*
Finger poppy mallow *(Callirhoe digitata)*
Flax *(Linum)*
Flowery scurfpea *(Psoralea floribunda)*

Fog fruit (or Lippia) *(Phyla cuneifolia)*
Four o'clock *(Mirabilis nyctaginea)*
Fringeleaf ruellia *(Ruellia humilis)*
Gaura *(Gaura longiflora)*
Gayfeather *(Liatris mucronata)*
Giant goldenrod *(Solidago gigantea)*
Grasses
   Big bluestem *(Andropogon gerardii)*
   Blue grama *(Bouteloua gracilis)*
   Buffalo grass *(Buchloe dactyloides)*
   Eastern gamagrass *(Tripsacum dactyloides)*
   Fun sedge *(Carex heliophilia)*
   Hairy grama *(Bouteloua hirsuta)*
   Indian grass *(Sorghastrum nutans)*
   Junegrass *(Koeleria pyramidata)*
   Little bluestem *(Andropogon scoparius)*
   Needlegrass *(Stipa spartea)*
   Prairie cordgrass *(Spartina pectinata)*
   Prairie dropseed *(Sporobolus heterolepis)*
   Purple three awn *(Aristida purpurea)*
   Scribner's panic grass *(Panicum scribnerianum)*
   Side oats grama *(Bouteloua curtipendula)*
   Switchgrass *(Panicum virgatum)*
   Threadleaf sedge *(Carex filifolia)*
   Western wheatgrass *(Agropyron smithii)*
Green antelopehorn *(Asclepias viridis)*
Green milkweed *(Asclepias viridiflora)*
Ground-plum milk-vetch *(Astragalus crassicarpus)*
Hairy gromwell *(Lithospermum carolinense)*
Heath aster *(Aster ericoides)*
Hemp dogbane *(Apocynum cannabinum)*
Hoary vervain *(Verbena stricta)*
Illinois bundleflower *(Desmanthus illinoensis)*
Illinois tickclover *(Desmodium illinoense)*
Jerusalem artichoke sunflower *(Helianthus tuberosa)*
Lambert crazyweed *(Oxytropis lambertii)*
Leadplant *(Amorpha canescens)*
Light poppy mallow *(Callirhoe alceoides)*
Long-beard hawkweed *(Hieracium longipilum)*

Low poppy mallow (Callirhoe involucrata)
Mugwort wormwood (Artemisia ludoviciana)
Narrowleaf bluet (Hedyotis nigricans)
Narrowleaf gromwell (Lithospermum incisum)
Narrowleaf milkweed (Asclepias stenophylla)
Noble goldenrod (Solidago speciosa)
Nodding lady's tresses (Spiranthes cernua)
Nuttall evolvulus (Evolvulus nuttallianus)
Old plainsman (Hymenopappus scabiosaeus)
Pale ragweed (Ambrosia artemisiifolia)
Pitcher's salvia (Salvia azurea)
Plume dalea (Dalea enneandra)
Prairie groundsel (Senecio plattensis)
Prairie spiderwort (Tradescantia occidentalis)
Prairie sunflower (Helianthus petiolaris)
Pussytoes (Antennaria neglecta)
Purple prairie clover (Dalea purpurea)
Rayless thelesperma (Thelesperma megapotamicum)
Roughleaf dogwood (Cornus drummondii)
Roundhead lespedeza (Lespedeza capitata)
Rush skeleton plant (Lygodesmia juncea)
Scarlet gaura (Gaura coccinea)
Scarlet globemallow (Sphaeralcea coccinea)
Shortstem spiderwort (Tradescantia tharpii)
Silverleaf scurfpea (Psoralea argophylla)

Slender lady's tresses (Spiranthes gracilis)
Slimflower scurfpea (Psoralea tenuiflora)
Small skullcap (Scutellaria parvula)
Small soapweed (or yucca) (Yucca glauca)
Snow-on-the-mountain (Euphorbia marginata)
Spanish needles (Bidens bipinnata)
Stiff sunflower (Helianthus rigidus)
Stiffleaf vetch (Vicia americana)
Sunshine rose (Rosa suffulta)
Tall eupatorium (Eupatorium altissimum)
Toothleaf evening primrose (Oenothera serrulata)
Tiny bluets (Hedyotis crassifolia)
Trailing wild bean (Strophostyles helvola)
Venus's looking-glass (Triodanis perfoliata)
Violet woodsorrel oxalis (Oxalis violacea)
Wavyleaf agoseris (Microseris cuspidata)
Wavyleaf thistle (Cirsium undulatum)
Western wild lettuce (Lactuca ludoviciana)
White prairie clover (Dalea candida)
Whorled milkweed (Asclepias verticillata)
Wild onion (Allium canadense)
Woolly croton (Croton capitatus)
Woolly Indian wheat (Plantago purshii)
Woolly loco (Astragalus mollissimus)
Yellow woodsorrel oxalis (Oxalis stricta)

Library of Congress Cataloging in Publication Data
Evans, Terry.
    Prairie: images of ground and sky.
    1. Prairie ecology—Kansas. 2. Prairies—Kansas.
I. Title.
QH105.K3E93   1986   574.5′2643′09781   85-28872
ISBN 0-7006-0287-9